Gi
Sugar & Spice!

WEST
SIDE
PUBLISHING

PHOTO CREDITS:

FRONT COVER: Jupiterimages

BACK COVER: Adams Picture Library (left); Aurora Photos (right)

Adams Picture Library; Aurora Photos; Heide Benser; Bettmann; Ben Bloom; Brand X Pictures; Per Breiehagen; Bubbles Photolibrary; Kimber Dahlquist; Dex Images, Inc.; Fox Photos; Rene Frederick; Greg Gerla; Getty Images; Hulton-Deutsch Collection; Image Club; Jose Luis Peleaz, Inc.; Jupiterimages; Ronnie Jaufman; Anna Kern; Elmar Krenkel; Lew Long; LWA-Dann Tardif; Roy Marsch; Don Mason; Ebby May; Kimmasa Mayama; Media Bakery; Eri Morita; Frank Muckenheim/Westend61; November; Jose Luis Pelaez; Popperfoto; Rob & Sas; H. Armstrong Roberts; David Roth; Norbert Schaefer; Shutterstock; Ariel Skelley; Arthur Steel; StockphotoPro; Steffen Thalemann; Ulf Huett Hilsson; Larry Williams; Win Initiative

West Side Publishing is a division of Publications International, Ltd.

Louis Weber, CEO
Publications International, Ltd.
7373 North Cicero Avenue
Lincolnwood, Illinois 60712

ISBN-13: 978-1-60553-541-8

ISBN-10: 1-60553-541-9

Manufactured in China.

8 7 6 5 4 3 2 1

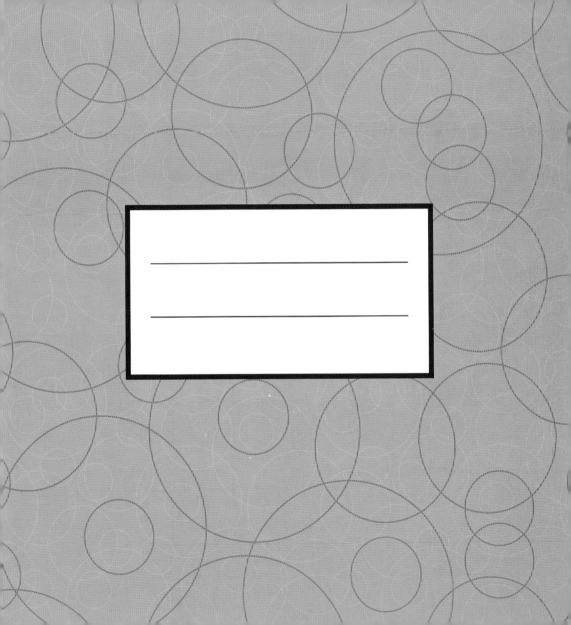

Girls Just Want to Have Fun!

Sugar and spice and everything nice—that's what little girls are made of. Right? Girls are often perceived as well-behaved, quiet creatures who play peacefully with their dolls. The people who think this must not be parents of girls!

You don't have to be demure and overly dignified to be a princess—and these girls prove it! By turns sassy, smart, bold, and playful, the girls featured in the photos and captions of *Girls: Sugar & Spice?* redefine what it means to be a "good girl." With infectious joy, they explore the world, competing in sports, making mischief, and yes, even playing with bugs on occasion.

At the park, at home, and around town, these girls are captured perfectly in their exuberance and abandon. From the aching sweetness of stopping to smell the flowers to the thrill of outdoor adventures to the joy of getting really dirty every once in a while, these photos capture the energy, excitement, and sheer fun of growing up as a girl. They may find themselves in a tight spot or a sticky situation (literally) now and again, but the charm and personality of these girls shine through. What are little girls really made of? A peek inside these pages will show you both the sugary and spicy sides of girlhood.

Maybe she'll MARRY into MONEY.

Sure, they're friends now. But wait until they have to SHARE a

BATHROOM!

Emily takes the phrase "BREAK THE ICE" a little too literally.

By morning, Julie would have her brother convinced that he was SHRINKING.

BAYWATCH—next generation

You're right—this is a GREAT
way to DRY your hair!

If they're all different, why don't I ever get one that tastes like MINT?

Amy finds out that
"PRETTY PLEASE WITH A
CHERRY ON TOP" really
does work.

After WINNING her first two matches, Leslie patiently waits for her next OPPONENT.

Kiss enough **FROGS** and you'll eventually find one that will CLEAN the **LILY PAD** without being asked.

Drifting apart isn't the same as *LETTING GO.*

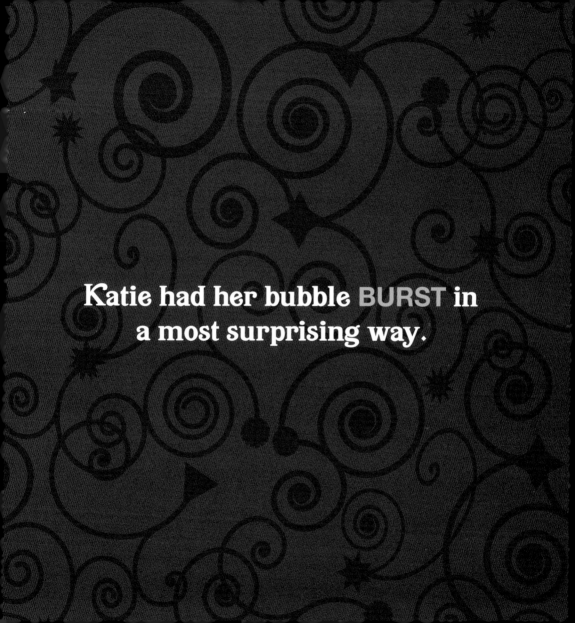

Katie had her bubble BURST in
a most surprising way.

Any way you look at it,
GIRLS RULE!

Moms know: The BIGGER the BUG, the more a boy likes you!

Does this underwear
make me look *FAT?*

I was told there would be BOYS here!

"What's up DOCK?" It's still not funny. Maybe you're saying it wrong.

BLENDING IN turned out to be a lot **HARDER** than Emma anticipated.

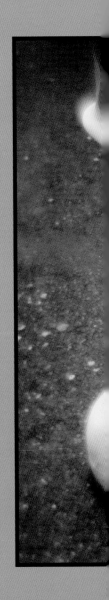

Sally's scheme to **HIDE** the rest of the muffin pans had definitely paid off.

Hey Mom! Did you know that SOME houses come with TWO bathrooms?!

I'd say she's more of a 34C.

SECONDS, anyone?

A woman's DESIRE for a DIAMOND RING begins early.

You'd do it too if you saw
what my little brother
DID in the BATHTUB.

NATURE calls!

A classic case of
BINGE and REGRET...

Between the two of us, we have the whole court COVERED.

Patty covered all the bases by *WISHING* **for A BABY SISTER, A PUPPY, or A BEACH BALL.**

You say that *NOW*, but once we're married, you'll be hogging this blanket.

Her parents hoped that by
the time Julia had grown into
the shoes, she'd have stopped
using the PACIFIER.

WORST. Pickpocket. EVER.

You know what they say:
It's important to be FLEXIBLE.

Sometimes, you've got to take STYLE RISKS to be a TRENDSETTER.

I'm guessing you don't
want to see the **DOG** then.

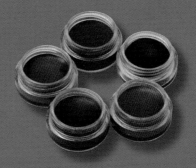

Like *YOU'VE* never had a **BAD HAIR DAY?**

**Whew, last one.
Now to get the DOGS.**

FREEDOM is so CLOSE
I can taste it.

The WRITING is on the wall, and it spells TIME-OUT.

Photographic evidence proves
that Little Red Riding Hood did,
in fact, have an OUTIE.

By the time she got to the spill, Gretta didn't have ANYTHING left to wipe it up with.

ENOUGH with the RA-RA-RA already!

Unable to control her own LAUGHTER, Ella's foray into the world of PRANK CALLING is only mildly successful.

Little did Frank know that
attendance at the Grandpa-
Granddaughter dance would
require MATCHING UPDOS

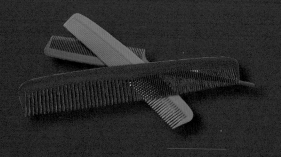

The diaper absorbency focus group results were inconclusive, most likely because the judges were looking at things UPSIDE DOWN.

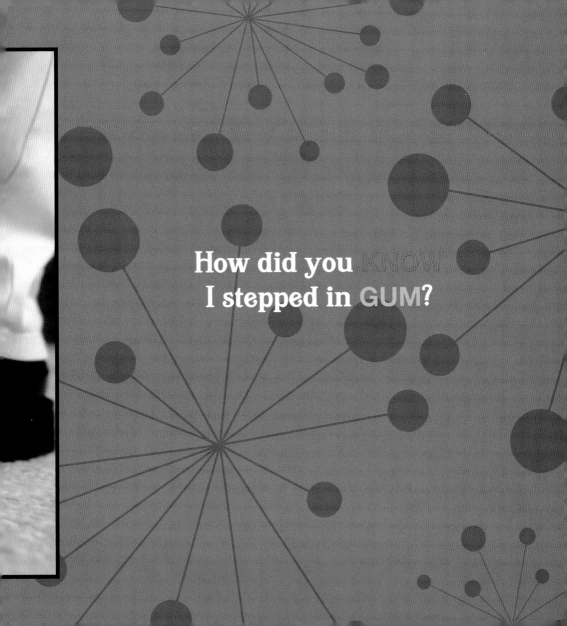

How did you KNOW
I stepped in GUM?

The sumo wrestler embarked on a successful second career as a **CHAMPION** at **BABY-CRYING CONTESTS** worldwide.

BOTTOMS up!

With appreciation for accordian music at an ALL-TIME LOW, Olivia's recitals were SURPRISINGLY well-attended.

Swinging can be a real HAIR-RAISING experience.

The business plan for Ricki's Rickshaw had been solid; it was the WEIGHT LIMITATION that proved to be its DOWNFALL.

If the girl won't come to the **BUBBLE BATH**, sometimes all a mom can do is bring the bubble bath to the girl.

I had NO idea I wasn't supposed to be in here. If only there were some kind of SIGN...

BATHERS ARE NOT ALLOWED ON THE FOUNTAIN

Stop moping. NOBODY gets to be the Swan Queen in their first year.

Clearly, attracting the rescue plane would require a PLAN B.

Never put all your sisters
in ONE basket. If you do,
there won't be anyone
left to carry it.

DISSATISFIED with her life,
Dena prepares to mail herself
to the Bahamas.

After her family moved to the country, time-outs weren't SO BAD anymore.

Polly won on melody,
but Isabel won on
SHEER VOLUME.

Hmm. Boots, check. Diaper, check. Nope, I don't think I'm **MISSING ANYTHING.**

STOP! **You're drinking all the profits.**

In the competition to see who could blow the candles out first, the birthday girl was totally **SHOVED** out of the running.

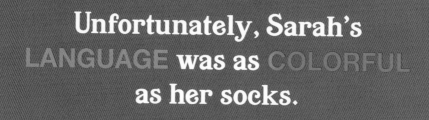

Unfortunately, Sarah's LANGUAGE was as COLORFUL as her socks.

WHAT THE...? Who is Inspector Number 12 and why is she leaving notes in my underpants?

After weeks of campaigning for a birthday with all the frills, Mara learned to be CAREFUL WHAT SHE WISHED FOR.

You're kidding...
it's been **DONE** before?

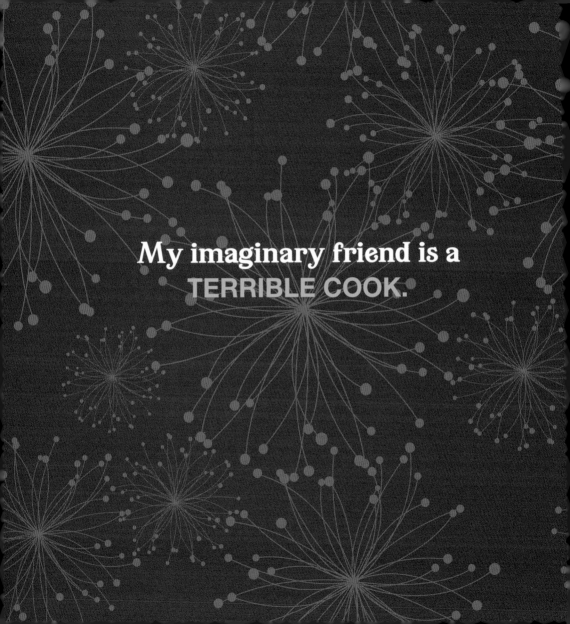

My imaginary friend is a
TERRIBLE COOK.

What do I have to do to get some SERVICE around here?

The recession had hit hard, but the children of the Palm Springs Preschool and Day Spa were determined to KEEP THE PLACE RUNNING.

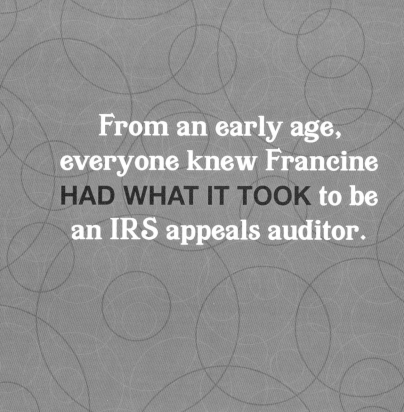

From an early age,
everyone knew Francine
HAD WHAT IT TOOK to be
an IRS appeals auditor.

Janie wasn't sure what was worse: the forced hike through the Arctic or the fact that her dad had forgotten her GLOVES.

Erica misunderstood when her mother told her to let her hair "AIR DRY."

What Mary Catherine lacked in TACT and DIPLOMACY, she made up for in CLARITY.

When her baby brother needed CHANGING, Priscilla found it best to wait outside.

If Maggie played her cards right, she would remain an ONLY CHILD.

[REDACTED] Angela will now dive 40 feet, blindfolded, into a bottomless tub of water! Correction: into a TUB OF WATER, BOTTOMLESS !

About the Authors

Wendy Burt-Thomas is being held against her will by a preschool/toddler tag team. She is forced to survive on little sleep, a house full of pink toys, and a diet of gummy worms. Her second mortgage is paying for her 4-year-old's ever-changing wardrobe.

Holli Fort got her start in fiction at an early age by making creative excuses to get out of homework. She has passed her skills to two little sisters, one niece, and countless cousins, and enjoys watching a new crop of female family members break the mold.

Formerly a little girl, **Kathryn Hammer** is currently a grown-up author, speechwriter, and executive communications consultant. She was never, ever naughty or mischievous, and none of the stories her many sisters and friends tell about her are true. At all.

Troy Higgins is a comedic author living in Charlotte, North Carolina. He knows a thing or two about little girls, saying, "I grew up with three older sisters. Try wearing their hand-me-down dresses and *not* learning a thing or two."

Chicago-based writer **Lyndsay Rush** credits her love of laughter and her overactive imagination to her mother, who taught her that just because you have to grow old doesn't mean you have to grow up. She loves spending time with her friends and family and still holds firmly to the belief that girls rule and boys drool.

Paul Seaburn thinks girls are funnier than boys, and he has had the pleasure of writing for a number of female comedians and speakers, as well as for almost-as-funny boys on television, radio, magazines, books, newspapers, and the Internet. Girls (and boys too) can read more about him at www.humorhandyman.com.

Contributing Writer: **John McNamee**